T0086542

PREDESTINED TO FULFILL A MISSION

A guide to help you figure out your calling and what "God" expects of you

ESSIE MOORE

authorHOUSE®

AuthorHouse™
1663 Liberty Drive
Bloomington, IN 47403
www.authorhouse.com
Phone: 833-262-8899

Published by AuthorHouse 09/07/2021

ISBN: 978-1-6655-3717-9 (sc)
ISBN: 978-1-6655-3718-6 (e)

Library of Congress Control Number: 2021918564

Print information available on the last page.

All scriptures were taken from the King James version of the Bible.

Contents

ACKNOWLEDGMENTS

I would like to thank everyone that has taken time out of your busy schedules to assist me with this mission that I have been assigned. This book has not been an easy task for me to write, but I know that God would not have assigned it to me, had he thought that I would not be able to complete it.

Thank you, to my husband Regenold Moore, for all your help. Throughout my life you have been an inspiration to me, by helping me to understand the bible and the scriptures that I have used in this book. You offered Prayer and told me to seek understanding and then let God give me direction in whatever I was wanting to convey to the reader. Thank you so much.

Another inspiration in my life has been my former Pastor, for your wisdom and understanding in guiding me through some of the obstacles and challenges that I've faced on this journey and to my daughter's for just being there when I needed to talk about what I should do next.

And for each and everyone that I have not mentioned, but helped in some way, thank you as well, I will never forget how thoughtful everyone was in making this book come alive and has helped me fulfill my calling, and from the bottom of my heart, Thank you.

Praying Time

Dear Lord,

Please hear my Prayer. I lift you up because you are my father in heaven and on earth, and there is no other name greater than the name of Jesus, your darling son that died on the cross for me, your darling son that gave his life for a wretch undone, needed healing and the chance to surrender all to you. I have prayed and now I understand. I thank you Lord, because you are God, and you are God all by yourself. You are Alpha and Omega, the Beginning, and the End, The Bright and Morning Star, the Rose of Sharon, the Lily of the Valley, you are Jehovah Jira-my Provider, and you are so much more. I thank you because you woke me up this morning and gave me a new start, I thank you because you was there when I needed a friend, you was there when I didn't think that I could make it, you was there through the good and the bad times, you was there when my fleshly body said no more, but the spiritual mind said, yes, Thank you Lord.

Thank you for the sunshine and the rain, thank you for putting your loving arms around me and letting me know each day that you love me because I am made in your image, and you would not leave me alone. In your "Word" you promised that you would not leave me comfortless and that you would send the Holy spirit to dwell amongst our earthly selves, thank you Lord. I love you, because you sent your son Jesus to die on that old rugged cross and bear the sins of the world just to save a wretch like me. I thank you and I love you Lord because you first loved me. You are my father and I adore you, you are my Way maker and I cannot survive without you, You are my shelter in the time of a storm, you are my rock in a weary land, you are my friend when I need a friend and because you live Lord, I can face tomorrow, because you live, I am clothed in my right mind, because you live I can get out of my bed by myself every morning and every day is a brand new day. Thank you, Lord, because you've taught me how to love those that despitefully use me, you've taught me how to love my friends and my enemy. Thank you for guiding me on the right path and helping me to design and put this book together to inspire and maybe help someone else. Asking you to bless the whole world and let them know that you are God and besides thee, there is none other. I pray all these blessings in your darling son Jesus name. Amen

"Be careful of nothing; but in everything by prayer and supplication with thanksgiving let your requests be made known unto God".
(Philippians 4:6 KJV)

"And I will pray the Father, and he shall give you another Comforter, that he may abide with you forever". (John 14:16 KJV)

"We love him, because he first loved us".
(I JOHN 4:19 KJV)

God to Be Praised for His Glorious Works
(Psalm 111 1-10 KJV)

"Praise ye the Lord. I will praise the
Lord with all my whole heart,
In the assembly of the upright,
and in the congregation.
The works of the Lord are great, sought out
of all of them that have pleasure therein.
His work is honourable and glorious:
and his righteousness endureth forever.
He hath made his wonderful
works to be remembered:
the Lord is gracious and full of compassion
He hath given meat unto them that fear him:
he will ever be mindful of his covenant.
He hath shewed his people the
power of his great works,
that he may give them the heritage of the heathen.
The works of his hands are verity and judgment.
all his commandments are sure.
They stand fast forever and ever.
and are done in truth and uprightness.
He sent redemption unto his people:

he hath commanded his covenant forever.
holy and reverend is his name.
The fear of the Lord is the beginning of wisdom:
a good understanding have all they
that do his commandments:
his praise endureth forever".
(Psalm 111 1-10 KJV)
AND Praise shall continually be in my mouth……

PREFACE

Life Thought's and Direction

To understand my mission, I have used scriptures and Bible stories, to help the reader get a better understanding what God has commissioned me to do. The people that are mentioned in this book, all had assignment's given to them by God. These assignments had to be fulfilled and through their experiences and their trials, I hope that you get a better understanding of what my story is all about.

This book is written with love, as a book of hope and inspiration to help guide you in whatever God has laid on your heart. I am using "Four Key Encounters", that God had with his children. It was Christ speaking to them, and through his command they were strongly inspired to do what they were assigned without question. (For example), maybe you are struggling with where you are to work in the church, you don't know what it is that God wants you to do, and you are confused about it. Believe it or not, I've been there, and I am telling you that if you listen to your heart and pray for peace and understanding, God will open the door for you, and you will find your place in the task that you have been assigned. Whether it is ushering, singing in the choir, evangelizing, youth director, choir president, etc., you will know where you are to work.

I pray that as you read you begin to understand and meditate on what God has commissioned you to do. Perform it with the boldness, believing that God is with you, and he will bring it to past, if; you just trust and believe in his word.

INTRODUCTION

This is my story, written to help, inspire, motivate, and send a message to someone else letting them know that God has not forsaken you, and that he is right there in their time of need and trouble. Know that whatever you are going through God can and will work it out for your good. He is the Creator of both heaven and earth and has given us an assignment to fulfill. Hopefully after reading my story, you will be able to find exactly what it is that God has empowered you to do.

I believe my commission was set before I was conceived in my mother's womb. It was already predestined by the Lord that I would write this book and complete everything that he has assigned to me. God knew my purpose before I even knew myself. This book is to uplift your spirits and your inner being and hopefully help you discover who you are and what God has anointed you to do.

Please feel free to use this book to study to help you find yourself through meditation and prayer. God sees everything that we do and hears everything that we say. May God Bless and Keep you.

"Behold I was shapen in iniquity; and in sin did my mother conceive me". (Psalm 51:5 KJV)

"Behold I stand at the door and knock if any man hears my voice, and open the door, I will come into him, and will sup with him, and he with me". (Revelation 3:20 KJV)

My Commission, "My Story"

When I was a young child my environment in the home was at first, a healthy environment. I had a mother and father who worked and kept our family together. I was the fifth child born to D.C. Randolph and Gracie Lee (Frazier) Walters. I had four siblings, two sisters and two brothers. My father was a roofer and my mother worked at a local cleaner, steaming, pressing, and laundering clothing. I remember having to go to work with her sometimes because she did not have a babysitter. When I reached the age of about seven years old, my father passed away. This put a great strain on my mother, and it impacted how my siblings and I lived the rest of our childhoods. After my father was laid to rest, my mother met another man, and I did not like him because he was very verbal and abusive. He was now living in our home and came home every day from work with the smell of liquor on his breathe. He smelled like oil, dirt, sweat, and metal and because he was an abusive man, my mother got knocked around by him all the time especially when the two of them were drinking. I do not remember a time that my real father ever hit or abused my mother., so this was something that as a child I did not understand, All I knew was that it was wrong for him to have physical altercations and hit my mother. The hitting and drinking went on until my oldest sister decided that she would remove me and my other sister from the home, I was nine years old at the time and my other sister was twelve, and soon after we moved out of the home, my mother was expecting another child, I would soon have a little sister, I would no longer be the baby of the family. My mother was pregnant by a man I hated. I know that "hate" is a strong word, and we must love everyone, but I had every reason to feel the way that I felt about this man. I was not a Christian at that time. I was merely a baby, so I did not know how to express my feelings, other than to say that I hated him.

So, since my mother was expecting a child, she continued in the relationship. Things got better and I was happy that I did not have to see the man that my mom had chosen for a partner, after the death of my father. Although we moved in with my oldest sister and her husband, my other sister, still was unhappy, and when she turned fifteen, she ran away from home to live with other family members. She said that she would be happier someplace else and hearing her speak those words made me sad again, because I did not want my sister to leave me. I did not go with her because I was only a scared child, and I knew even at the age of nine that the best place for me was with people who cared about my well-being.

I went to school every day just like normal kids growing up and was very happy. Things were pretty good as the years went by, I would talk on phone to my friends, play with my dolls, listen to music, sing along with my 8-track tapes, listen to the R&B songs that my oldest sister and her husband use to play, and go to movies. After the sun went down, the neighborhood kids would come out, and we would mark the street with white chalk and make squares and play hopscotch. Those are all good memories.

At the age of seventeen, I met a very handsome young boy. He was eighteen and could play basketball like crazy. He was tall, dark, and distinguished looking, his physique was perfect. I knew when I met him, that he would be the love of my life. He and I dated for over a year and then we married. This is when my life took another turn, I had to grow up a little faster, because I was about to become someone's wife. When I was eighteen years old, I married the love of my life, and I became a hard-working certified nurse's assistant. Later, the place where I was employed offered me the opportunity to continue my education and become a licensed vocational nurse, which I was not successful at becoming. The nursing class was very crowded, and there were so many applicants to choose from.

Although my score was acceptable, there were others who scored higher than I did, so I wasn't accepted, into the program. I believe that God had another plan for me to help people, which was to become a cosmetology instructor. But this did not happen for me right away.

I had been walking in my true purpose all my life, but I just did not realize that what God had for me was for me. It was challenging for me to complete one task without starting another. I've always felt like I should be doing more and more, because I am not a quitter. I would complete one task and then began another one before I could finish the first one. As far back as I can remember, I have always been like this, little did I know that I had some other hurdles to overcome. The love of my life and I filed for a separation, in 1976. I continued to work as a certified Nurse's assistant and earn money to live on.

After several years as a certified nurse assistant, I decided that I wanted to be more financially stable, so after, my husband of two and a half years and I divorced, I joined the United States Army. I signed on for three years, and although I only completed a short term of it and earned an honorable discharge. I was then recognized as a veteran and was hired at a boiler makers' plant. This plant was one of the highest paid companies in the area in which I lived, and only five or six women, with men making up most workers.

So, once again, God had his hands on me. When we are young, we sometimes classify good things that come to us as the results of being "lucky", but now I know that it wasn't luck. "I was blessed". I worked for this company for about five and a half years, making very good money. However, I still didn't feel complete. I felt like I could do more, and I yearned for more, not just for material, but for a stronger relationship with the Lord.

After I had worked for this company, a short while, God placed my prior husband

back in my life. We started dating and remarried in 1979. Again, I believe that it was in God's plan for this to happen. I continued working after we married, while I was still working God paved the way for me to go to Beauty school to become a licensed cosmetologist. My husband told me that if I completed the cosmetology program, he would build me a business to operate as a stylist, and guess what, he was not slack on his promise.

After I remarried and begun school, God proceeded to open paths for me, and all I had to do was walk through them. He presented the opportunity for me to become employed at an even better place to work. I was hired by a local company, as an assistant productions operator and my compensation for this company by far surpassed what I was directly making. I was so pleased, at what God was doing in my life.

This is when I really began to realize that God was Blessing me beyond measures. I believe that I had found favor with the lord because he was so good to me. I started Praying even more and asking God to show me direction and give me more understanding of the scriptures. I had something tugging on me that would not let go. I kept seeking more and more of this man called "Jesus". I believed in the bible, went to Sunday school, attended bible class and church on Sunday, but I did not know God like I really wanted to. I wanted a personal relationship with him, so my husband begins to kneel in prayer together at bedtime.

According to Matthew 7:7-8 (KJV), reads "Ask, and it shall be given; seek, and ye shall find; knock, and it shall be opened unto you: For everyone that asketh receiveth; and to him that knocketh it shall be opened".

My husband was ordained as a Deacon at the church where we both attended. I served the Lord by singing in the choir. Most people who heard me sing said that my voice was anointed, and that when I sang, it was as if I were telling a story, because they could visualize what I was singing about.

So, after a while, I found out I was having a child, which was a blessing at 32 years old. We had attempted to have a child previously, but my body was not strong enough. I had already suffered the loss of a child, but this time was different, and I felt the

Lord was with us. It was palpable in my spirit. As a result, I was expecting once more and in hopes that we did not repeat what had happened in the past, which was to suffer the loss of another child.

According to, 2 Timothy 1:7 (KJV),
"God hath not given us the spirit of fear, but of power, and of love, and of a sound mind."

We held on to this scripture and was steadfast in God's Word that he was going to see us through this storm from the beginning to the end. As a result, we prayed nonstop every day and night. God then brought us to a doctor who was able to assist us; he said that if I could carry the baby for three months without going into labor, he might be able to assist us. He stated that he could perform a surgery, that would allow me to be able to carry the baby to term.

As the month's passed, what do you think happened? We completed the task! Our newborn baby weighed in at a healthy 9 pounds, 12 ounces, Brittany Nichole was a baby girl, and she was beautiful; this was yet another blessing that had come our way, Hallelujah.

Our faith grew stronger by the day. As our

daughter approached the age of two, God said, "Now I am going to elevate you a little higher," and he blessed me with another job.

A position that I had prayed and gone to beauty school for. I was hired at a community college as Instructor of cosmetology. I was in shock, and I never will forget how all these things transpired. Now, I had an even better opportunity to earn more wages and devote more time to the Lord, because the college was closed on weekends. I did not have to work rotating shifts. When I was hired at the college, I met the requirements for hiring, however, I did not have a degree, so, the college gave me time to my first degree, which was my Associates degree.

I was so happy and could not believe that I had accomplished such a goal. I was surrounded by positive role models and friends, so I decided that I would go back to college and get my second degree, which was my bachelor's degree. It felt like I was on a roller coaster and could not get off it. After completing my Bachelors, I then decided that I wanted to get my master's degree in Education and guess what; "I did", however, I am beginning to feel drained of my energy from attending so many classes, but I didn't quit, I kept pushing myself to go farther.

Shortly after that, I started on my Doctorates degree at an online university and worked hard toward it. I am a First-generation graduate of my family, and I am so, so proud of God working in my life, and out of all my trials and accomplishments, I still have not completed or achieved what God has for me. I am predestined to complete this mission, and I will not rest until it is finished.

When God has his hands on you, you cannot give up, if you have the faith of a mustard seed that you're going to get through it, and believe that God will be there for you, you will succeed. There is a passage in the (KJV) bible, that I often think about because it keeps me content in whatever I am doing for the Lord. In his "Word" he reminds me that I never want to give up on him, because he won't give up on me.

"Now to Him who is able to do exceedingly abundantly above all that we ask or think, according to the power that works in us".

(Ephesians 3:20 KJV)

"I am the vine ye are the branches, He that abideth in me and I in him, the same bringeth forth much fruit, for without me ye can do nothing". (John 15:5 KJV)

Because we have been altered and reborn, this passage suggests that "God" can do incredible things in our lives through his power that works in us. If you stay on the Lord's side, you will not go astray, and your life will be fruitful; nevertheless, if you tear yourself away from the vine, you will have nothing, and you will die, for if the fruit has fallen off the tree how can it remain plump. We are like a dead tree planted by the rivers of water.

Key Encounter: Inspirational I

Jesus and John, the Baptist

John the Baptist had been summoned to be a messenger before Jesus started his ministry. John was going about telling people that someone was coming greater than he, he was speaking of Jesus coming. John was preparing the way for Jesus. While Jesus was going about Baptizing people telling them to repent of their sins. John told the people that someone was coming that would be baptizing with spirit and fire. John told the people that he only baptized with water.

Jesus quickly appeared one day as John was baptizing at the river of Jordan and told John that he wanted to be baptized. So, John baptized Jesus because it was God's will, and when he was baptized, the Holy spirit descended upon him, and a voice came from heaven and said you are my beloved son in whom I am well pleased.

John did not want to baptize Jesus because he

felt like Jesus should be baptizing him, but he had to because God had already assigned the baptism of his beloved son. We should remember that when God tells us to do something we should do it without hesitation. We should pray and ask God for direction to carry out his will. Like John, we feel unqualified to do some things that God ask us to do, but if we first seek his face and pray, then we will hear from him. Jesus' baptism was a symbol of obedience and a sign of repentance.

When you seek him and pray for direction and understanding, God will answer. He does not speak to you in an audible voice or appear to you as a human being, but he uses others to get his message across to you. He will speak to your heart, and you will know that is the good Lord. He tugs on your mind, and he won't leave you alone. This tugging and burning desire are how I know that the good Lord is dealing with me. I know his voice and I trust him. I am blessed and highly favored. I can confide in him, and he will not tell anyone, he is my friend, he is my everything, and when I pray to him in sincerity, I know that he is going to answer. He is my salvation, my rock, and my Lord. After reading this short version of Jesus and

John the Baptist, please don't feel less worthy like John and miss out on what God has appointed you to do. John prayed and followed God's command.

John Baptizing Jesus

"I have baptized you with water, but; he will baptize you with the Holy Spirit". (Matthew 1:8 KJV)

Key Encounter: Inspirational II

Walking in your Destiny

(Numbers 23:19 KJV)
"God is not a man that he should lie, neither the son of man, that he should repent: hath, he said, and shall not do it." or hath he spoken, and shall he not make it good"?

Walking in your destiny.

Have you ever considered what that means?

I have, and to me it means that God has a specific purpose just for you. It has been

laid out and designed according to his WORD, that he cannot lie.

"Let's take a look further".

When everything started evolving in my life, even as a young child, I could not comprehend what the Lord wanted me to do. And being a child at seven years old, I don't think that I even thought about God at all, let alone having an assignment appointed by him. I was a baby that needed hugs and kisses, someone to tell me that I was loved. Not realizing that God was there all the time.

As I grew older, I became more interested in learning more about God's Word and why I was so nervous and had butterflies in my stomach. I became a member of a church not far from where I grew up. The elders in this church would shout, sing, and cry out to God, but I couldn't understand why I didn't feel the same way they did. I used to enjoy going to church because it was interesting to see people I didn't know.

We used to go to other churches and sing, "I loved to sing," and then the pastor would take us to a drive-thru for hamburgers and a drink. That, I suppose, was his way of expressing his gratitude for us accompanying him to church. After a few years, I realized that my mission was to offer aid and direction to others by using my gifts, singing, and teaching.

According to the Bible, we are all born with different gifts that are to be used in different ways and set apart from one another. When you discover what God has planned for you, you are to utilize it to praise him rather than to be ashamed of it.

I feel chills and goosebumps every time I think about how my life has transformed, because my life right now couldn't be any better.

The Bible tells us that we are born with different gifts, and they are all to be used in different ways and set apart from anyone else. When you discover what it is that God has for you, then you are supposed to use it to glorify him and not be ashamed.

I needed to figure out what my mission was, and when I did, I learned that it was God working things out for my good, and what Satan meant for my bad, God turned into something positive.

I wasn't ready to shift to a higher level until he (God) was ready; he was preparing me for it, but my immaturity as a Christian meant I didn't recognize his voice. I wasn't prepared to take fruit from a tree that hadn't been manicured. As a result, God continued to work on me, instilling his Word in my heart. My gut felt like it was going to explode at moments, and my mind was not resting on the things that he had appointed for me to do I wanted to tell someone, what was happening to me, thinking this would help them, and hoping they would not ridicule me.

I am reminded of Jonah being sent on a mission

from the Lord. He was an Israelite whom God had called to be a Prophet. God had commissioned Jonah to go to Nineveh and tell them of their wickedness and that he was not pleased with the way they were living. Jonah did not want to perform this mission for some reason, I guess, he was just being hardheaded for whatever reason, so he fled to Tarshish, a region across the sea to flee from the presence of the Lord. Jonah then boarded a ship with some other men, and after Jonah boarded the ship, it started to rock and sway, it was disturbed by the winds that God has caused to come upon them because of Jonah's disobedience. Soon after, the men got scared and threw Jonah overboard, because they thought that he had bought evil to them. When Jonah was cast overboard God caused a fish to swallow him, and there he remained for three days and three nights. During the period that he was in the belly of the whale, Jonah repented and cried out to God in prayer and the Lord heard him, and at that moment God caused the whale to vomit up Jonah on dry land. Jonah was again assigned the same mission, and this time, he did as God had instructed him to do. So, he went to Nineveh telling the people what God wanted them to know.

When I think about the times that the Lord kept tugging at me to do things, I just ignored him, because I did not recognize that it was him until after, he fixed it so that I could not sing anymore. This happened in a way that I never figured it would happen. My husband and I belonged to a church, but it was hard to sing in a choir or sing period, due to lack of communication from everyone.

I wanted to sing, but the musician was limited to the type of music that was available, that I knew I was supposed to deliver to the congregation. As a result, I became dissatisfied and quit singing in the choir. Although, I wasn't singing in the choir, my heart was burning on the inside, because I had a calling on my life which was to minister to people through singing songs. My voice was anointed, whenever I sang, I felt the presence of the Holy Spirit on the inside of me.

People would ask me to sing, but I wouldn't. If I didn't have the right type of music, I would not sing, whenever, I was asked. So, soon after God fixed it so that I could sing, and the only way that I could sing, was to join the choir and sing with the musician that was already appointed to play at that time. I finally realized that, when it was time God would

Bless the church with whomever he pleased. I am still struggling with this call on my life, because I know that the only way, that I am going to be able to truly sing, is do it Gods' way, and surrender to him.

Have you ever considered your life's mission, or what you're supposed to accomplish for Christ, or what you enjoy doing, or perhaps you've discovered that one or two things that set you apart from others, and you've had a lot of fun doing it? If that's the case, it's possible that's what you're intended to be doing. It's not like God is going to tap you on your back or speak to you in an audible voice and tell you, "This is what you are supposed to do", No, he does not appear to you like that. He simply speaks to your heart, and you will identify and recognize him and know that it is the Good Lord, and you must obey his voice.

I had a friend, who was trying to figure out, if it was her wanting to do what pleased her, or if it was the Holy spirit trying to get her attention. So, when God is ready for you to accomplish something, you'll know it's him calling to you because his voice isn't like ours or how we're used to hearing people speak. He talks to our hearts and it won't leave you alone; it's like a burning need from within; for me, the words kept repeating themselves in my thoughts over and over, telling me to obey him. This was my encounter with him; the Lord would not leave me alone, so I had to do what he desired, and writing this book was part of that task.

I'm reminded of Jonah throughout my walk with the Lord. He needed to stay focused on his mission and complete the assignment that God had given him. You don't say, "I'm not going to do it," when the Lord prepares you to do something or have a calling on your life. You do it. God has a way of capturing your attention in a variety of ways. Your mind will be disturbed, he will speak to your heart, you will be uncomfortable in many ways.

Key Encounter: Inspirational III

Wandering in the Wilderness

I wonder how Moses felt when God told him to deliver his people from Pharoah. Did Moses ask himself who does God think that I am, to perform such a miracle.........Moses did just that, he did not think that he could carry out such a mission, so he doubted himself.

According to the book of (Exodus 4:10 KJV), "Moses said unto the LORD, O my Lord, I am not eloquent, neither heretofore, nor since thou hast spoken unto thy servant: but I am slow of speech, and of a slow tongue".

Moses spoke those words to God, because he had been assigned a mission to fulfill, and did not believe that he could do it, because of his speech and slow tongue. He even asked the Lord to send Aaron in his place. Moses asked the Lord, who do I tell them that sent me,

"And God said unto Moses, I AM THAT I AM: and he said, thus shalt thou say unto the children of Israel, I AM hath sent me unto you". (Exodus 3:14 KJV)

Moses was to go to Egypt and tell Pharoah that God said to let his people go. The story goes on and on, that after so many Plagues was placed in the land of Egypt, and on Pharoah he finally decided to let them go. Let's Take a closer look at the plagues listed in this book, I am only summarizing nine of the plaques.

Moses, Aaron, and the Israelites started on their journey in the wilderness. After traveling for so many days and nights they begin to complain, because they had gotten hungry, so God gave them Manna, which was food for them, each morning it was laid on the ground for them to eat.

They were angry at Moses for their conditions, but since God had told Moses to take the plight out of Egypt, he had no other choice but to obey God. After, the children of Israel wandered for forty days and forty nights, through all their suffering, trials and tribulations, the Lord brought them out of a situation that no other could do, he parted the Red Sea and let the Israelites pass and when Pharoah and his army tried to go through the waters the sea swallowed them up and his entire army drowned.

Moses at the Red Sea

This illustration was used to illustrate that no matter what you are going through, God can help you get through it. If God gives you a mission, you will carry it out. Moses tried to back out of what God had commanded him to do, but he couldn't since God had already chosen him to carry out his mission. Aaron, Moses' brother, had a mission from God as well, but the almighty God desired Moses for a specific task.

I'm not sure why God chose Moses to carry out his will, but I'm confident he understood the significance of such a high calling. When God prepares us for a task, we must complete it. It may take years to complete that task, but I am confident that as a Christian, you will complete it.

I am confident that whatever God has planned for you to do in your life will be fulfilled. Moses brought the people to the Promised Land, and he was permitted to peer over the border, but he was not allowed to cross because of his disobedience. Moses remained solid in his belief in what the Lord had instructed him to do. That's what we're supposed to do, and we're not supposed to be ashamed of it.

SUMMARY OF THE "NINE PLAGUES"

The Plaque of Blood

The Lord was speaking to Moses and told him that Pharoah's heart is stiff, and he refuses to let the people go. He told him to go to Pharoah in the morning, and go out and stand by the river water, Moses was to take the staff or rod that he normally carried in his hand and let Pharoah, and his people see that God turned the rod into a serpent. And Moses was to say unto them that God told him to deliver the message to Pharoah was to let his people go, so that they could be free to serve him in the wilderness, but Pharoah still refused to obey God's command from Moses.

So, God said, because of your disobedience, you will know that I am the Lord, I will strike the rod that is in my hand upon the water of the river, and it shall turn into blood. And in that river, the fish shall die, and the river water will smell of stink, and the Egyptians will be reluctant to drink of the river water. Then the Lord spoke to Moses to tell Aaron, to take the rod

and stretch it out over the Egyptian waters,

streams, rivers, ponds, and pools that they may all turn to blood. That blood would flow throughout Egypt from vessels of wood and in stone. Moses did as God commanded and Aaron followed through with what Moses had instructed him to do.

He raised up the rod over the waters of the river and smote it, so that Pharoah and all his army was in plain sight to view what was taking place, that the waters had indeed turned to blood. When Moses and Aaron followed through with the Lord's command the fish died that was in the river, the Egyptians could not drink the water, and blood was throughout the land of Egypt. The magicians even tried to make magic and reverse what the Lord had done, but to no avail they were not successful in doing, so. So, Pharoah's heart became even more stiff, and he went into his palace. The Egyptians waddled around in the river to find water to drink, but they could not undo the plaque that God had set upon them.

What do you think?

Question: Do you think that Pharoah should have learned from this lesson? Y or N

This was a very hard lesson for Pharoah and his people to learn, but when God tells you to do something, it is best to do it without ceasing. Pharoah caused a great plaque to be placed on himself and his people.

Record your thoughts:

____

____

____

____

____

____

____

____

____

____

____

____

The Plaque of Frogs

The Lord spoke to Moses and told Moses to go tell Pharoah and tell him, to let my people go, so that they may be able to serve me. "And if he refuses to let them go, tell him I will strike all the borders with frogs, and the river shall bring forth frogs abundantly, which shall go up and come into thine house, and into thy bedchamber, and upon thy bed, and into the house of thy servants, and upon thy people, and into thine ovens, and into thy kneading troughs". (Exodus: 8:3 KJV).

He said that he would have frogs come upon them and all his servants. So, the Lord spoke to Moses and told Moses to tell Aaron, to stretch forth thine hand with the rod in it over the streams, rivers and ponds and cause frogs to come upon the land of Egypt.

"And the frogs shall come up both on thee, and upon thy people, and upon all thy servants." (Exodus 8:4 KJV)

So, Aaron did stretch out his hand over the waters of Egypt and the frogs came up and covered the land of Egypt. Once the frogs were upon the land of Egypt the magicians tried to do what they could to interfere with their enchantments, but they could not stop the plaque because the Lord was too powerful for them to do anything, their tricks of magic did not work.

At this point Pharoah seemed to be giving into the Lord, so Pharoah called for Moses and Aaron and told them to ask the Lord to remove the plaque of frogs from him, and his people, and he will let the people go, so they can make sacrifice to the Lord. "And Moses said to Pharaoh, Glory over me: when shall I intreat for thee, and for thy servants, and for thy people, to destroy the frogs from thee and thy houses, that they may remain in the river only"? (Exodus 8:9 KJV). Again, Moses and Aaron went and pleaded to God to remove the plague of frogs, and God did, only for Pharoah, to again, go back on his word.

What do you think?

Question:

1. Do you think that it was fair to Moses for Pharoah to go back on his word, after Moses cried out to the Lord to remove the frogs from Pharoah, and do you think that Pharoah thought that he was right in his decision? Y or N

Record your thoughts:

____

____

____

____

____

____

____

____

____

____

____

____

The Plaque of Gnats

This plaque comes after the Plaque of frogs, which Pharoah could have been spared from, but due his disobedience and reluctance to let God's people go, God sent this plague to them. So, the Lord sent another Plaque, and this time he sent Gnats. The Lord is still telling Moses to tell Pharoah to let his people go, and because Pharoah keeps refusing, the Lord told Moses' to tell Aaron to stretch out his rod and strike the dust of the earth, that there will be lice throughout all the land of Egypt, and he did.

And as always Pharoah's magicians with their magical tricks tried to bring forth lice, but they could not. Lice was now upon man and beast. After the magicians used their witty enchantments to bring forth lice and failed, they told Pharoah that it was the finger of God. So Pharoah was again in sorrow and his heart was still hardened and he did not surrender to God. Here again, Pharoah has gone back on his word.

"And the Lord said unto Moses,Say unto
Aaron, Stretch out thy rod,and smite the
dust of the land, that it may become lice
throughout all of the land of Egypt".
Exodus 8:16 (KJV)

What do you think?

Question:

1. Do you believe that the magicians, believe that they could really overpower "God" with their enchantments?

Ask Yourself, (Y) or (N)

Record your thoughts:

Plaque of Flies

Again, God is trying to get Pharoah to let his people go. So, the Lord says to Moses, I want you to rise early in the morning and go stand before Pharoah and tell him once again to let my people go, so they may serve me. And, if Pharoah does not let them go, he is going to send another plaque to them, he is going to send swarms of flies upon Pharoah and his servants and people. The houses of the Egyptians will be full of flies and the ground, wherever they may be.

The Lord told Moses that he would save the land of Goshen, in which my people live, that they will not be affected by the flies, so that they will know that I am Lord during the earth. He told Moses's that he will put a separation between my people, and thy people, and it shall be a sign. Because Gods word is fulfilling, he did what he said he was going to do. Flies entered Pharoah's house, his servants' houses, and all the land of Egypt was corrupted by the swarms, and again, "Pharaoh called for Moses and Aaron, and said, go ye, sacrifice to your God in the land".

And Moses said, it is not meet so to do; for we

shall sacrifice the abomination of the Egyptians to the lord our God: lo, shall we sacrifice the abomination of the Egyptians before their eyes, and will they not stone us"? (Exodus 25-26 KJV).

So, Moses said to Pharaoh we will go out for a three-day journey in the wilderness, and sacrifice to the Lord, as he has commanded us to do. Pharoah told Moses that he would let them go, but not to go too far away. Pharoah wanted Moses to ask God again to remove the plague from the land. Moses responded to Pharoah and said that he would go, but if he does ask God, he must not deal deceitfully any more in not letting the people go to sacrifice to the Lord.

So, Moses went and cried to the Lord and the Lord heard Moses and removed the swarms of flies from Pharoah and there was none. Pharoah hardened his heart and would not let the people go.

What do you think?

Question:

Was it fair to Pharoah's people, to hold them, until after Moses cried to God again, knowing that Pharoah was not going to free them? (Y) or (N)

Why do you think that Pharoah, that each time that "God" brought a plague on Pharoah, he would say, that he would let the people go, and then change his mind? Was he trying to outsmart "God", What do you think?

Record your thoughts:

The Plaque of Livestock

The Lord told Moses, to go to Pharoah and tell him, that he said let his people go, so that they may serve him. And if Pharoah refuses to let them go, he told Moses to tell him that his hand would be upon their cattle in the field, their horses, their asses, camels, oxen, and sheep. And they would suffer. He told Moses, to tell Pharoah, that he would divide the cattle of Israel, and of Egypt, and that nothing out of the land of Israel would die during this time, but cattle would die in the land of Egypt. "And the Lord appointed a set time, saying, tomorrow the Lord shall do this thing in the land". (Exodus 9:5 KJV). So, God brought this plague upon Pharoah and the land of Egypt. Although Pharoah soon saw that none of the Israelites' cattle had died, but his heart remained stiff, and he refused to let the Egyptians serve the Lord. God was ready to send another plaque to Pharoah, his slaves, and all of Egypt, because Pharoah had not yet learnt his lesson.

The Plaque Boils

So, God once again told Moses and Aaron to take a handful of ashes and sprinkle it toward heaven, in sight of Pharoah. This dust was to become small dust in the land of Egypt and boils and sores will come upon man and beast throughout the land. Moses and Aaron did as they had been instructed to do, and the plague came, just as the Lord had said, it would happen. Even the magicians had boils and sores all over them, so, that they could not stand before Moses. And Pharoah's heart was still stiff.

God commanded Moses to get up early the next morning and tell Pharoah to release my people so that they may serve me. The Lord would send plaques to Pharoah, Egypt, and all his slaves this time. God was unleashing a scourge across the land. Moses was to warn them that God will smite them with disease and cut them off from the rest of the world.

What do you think?

Question:

1. Why do you think that Pharoah was being so rebellious to God, and Why? do you think that God should have kept repeatedly warning him?
2. Why do you think that Moses kept following God's command to keep returning to Pharoah crying out to God?
3. Why do you think that Pharoah had not learned his lesson?

Ask Yourself, (Y) or (N) What do you think?

Record your thoughts:

____

____

____

____

____

____

____

The Plague of Hail

Pharoah's heart was still hardened. The Lord said that he would send another plaque, he was going to cause it to rain very heavily, and the hail would be very severe, such as Egypt has not seen The Lord told Moses to tell the people of Egypt to gather up their cattle and all that they have in the field and every man and beast, get them to safety because everything else that is found in the field shall not be brought home, and everything in the path of the storm would die. Those that feared the Lord (Pharoah's servants) and his cattle went into their houses. And there was some that did not fear the word of the Lord, they left their cattle in the field.

The Lord had given them a chance to surrender to him, but since they did not, he told Moses to stretch his hands toward heaven, so that the hail would begin in the land of Egypt upon man, upon beast and every herb in the field throughout the land of Egypt. So, under God's instructions Moses stretched out his rod toward heaven and sent hail, and fire ran along the ground, and it hailed upon Egypt. And there was none like it before, the hail stuck every tree and all that was in the land, it was a great storm like never.

The children of Israel were saved from this storm, but only in the land of Goshen. Then Pharoah again called for Moses and Aaron, and said that he had sinned, and that the Lord is righteous, and he and his people were wicked. He asked Moses to go to the Lord once again, and ask him, that there be no more thunder and hail.

Pharoah told Moses that he would let him travel, but don't stay gone too long. Moses responded and told Pharoah that as soon as he is out of the city, he will spread his hands unto the Lord, and the thunder and hail shall cease, but as for you and your servants, you still will not fear the Lord. Moses spoke these words to Pharoah, because he gone back on his word so many times before. Pharoah acted at times as if he was bargaining with the Lord. So, Moses had completed his task assigned to him by the Lord and after it was complete Pharoah hardened his heart again.

What do you think?

Question:

1. Do you think that God should just go ahead and destroy Pharoah, and his people or should he keep giving him another chance? Y or N
2. Do you feel that Pharoah was bargaining with the Lord? Y or N
3. Why were the children of Israel saved from the storm, but only in the land of Goshen?

Record your thoughts:

____

____

____

____

____

____

____

____

____

____

The Plague of Locusts

The Lord tells Moses to go to Pharoah because he has hardened his heart, as well as the hearts of his slaves, so that the Lord can show these things to him. God desired for Pharoah and all of Egypt's people to recognize him and understand that he is the only and real God.

"And Moses and Aaron went to Pharoah and said unto him, thus saith the Lord God of Hebrews, how long wilt thou refuse to humble thyself before me? Let my people go, that they may serve me". (Exodus 10:3 KJV).

And God commanded Moses and Aaron to tell Pharoah that if he didn't let them go, he would send a locust plague, and the world would be covered in them, so densely that they wouldn't be able to see.

They'll devour whatever is left over from the hail, as well as any trees that sprout from the field.

The Lord said to tell Pharoah that the locust will fill their houses, and the houses of their servants, and the Egyptians houses, it will be a day that they have never seen. So, Moses turns away and went out from Pharoah.

"Pharoah's servants ask the question, how long shall this man be a snare to us? Let the men go, that they may serve the Lord their God; knowest thou not yet that Egypt is destroyed". And Moses and Aaron were brought to Pharoah again, and he said unto them, Go, serve the Lord your God: but who are they that shall go? And Moses said We will go with our young and our old, with our sons and with our daughters, with our flocks and with our herds will we go; we must hold a feast unto the Lord. And he said unto them, Let the Lord be so with you, as I will let you go, and your little ones: look to it; for evil is before you". (Exodus: 7-10 KJV)

So, they left, and the Lord said to Moses stretch out your hand over the land of Egypt for the locust will come up over the land and eat everything. And Moses followed God's command and the locust came and devoured the land of Egypt. Then, Pharoah again calls on Moses and Aaron to plead to the Lord on his behalf. He told Moses that he had sinned against the Lord your God and against you. So, Moses then goes unto the Lord again and ask him to remove the locust from the land, so God turned a mighty strong west wind and cast them into the red sea, and no locust remained in Egypt. But the Lord Hardened Pharoah's heart again, so that he would not let the people go.

What do you think?

Question:

1. Why do you think that God kept hardening Pharoah's heart? Was this fair to Pharoah?

Y or N

Record your thoughts:

___

___

___

___

___

___

___

___

___

___

___

___

___

The Plaque of Darkness

God tells Moses to stretch out his hand toward heaven because there may be darkness and even gloom felt over Egypt in this Plaque. As a result of Moses stretching out his hand, Egypt went black. For three days, the Egyptians were unable to see each other, but Israel had light and was able to see.

So, Pharoah called unto Moses and told him to go serve the Lord but leave your flocks and herds and take the little ones with him. Moses told Pharoah that he must give sacrifices and burnt offerings to sacrifice unto the Lord. According to the bible, he said that,

"Our cattle also shall go with us; there shall not a hoof be left behind; for thereof must we take to serve the LORD our God; and we know not with what we must serve the LORD, until we come thither". But the Lord hardened Pharaoh's heart so that he would not let the people go. Pharoah said unto him, get thee from me, take heed to thyself, see my face no more, for in that day thou seest my face thou shalt surely die. And Moses said, thou have spoken well, I will see thy face again no more". (Exodus 10: 26-29 KJV)

What do you think?

Question:

1. Do you feel like Pharoah is giving up by telling Moses to leave and take the little ones?

Y or N

2. How many days did Egypt remain black?
3. Why was there light in the land of Israel?

Record your thoughts:

____

____

____

____

____

____

____

____

____

____

____

Conclusion of the Nine Plagues

Due to disobedience from the people in Egypt God made darkness fall on these people through pain and suffering. He sent all kinds of pestilence and plaques on these people, but their hearts were hardened, and they did not want to change. God knew that he was going to cause a great tribulation to come upon them, but he kept on giving them chance after chance. Although the plaques were many, God was still offering them a chance to renew their minds and turn from their wicked ways. Through the reading of the Bible, and with me praying for an understanding of the scriptures, I have no doubt that God is going to come back and get his children and that we are all going to face a just God one day. We will be called one by one to face his judgment.

I have learned that when the Lord calls you and gives you an assignment. Then that has set your Mission in place, and you are to seek after whatever it is that he wants you to do. Pray for understanding that he might reveal to what you are to do. We are mere vessels used by God to help save someone else and tell them of his goodness and his mercy. God gave Moses an assignment, and Moses had to honor that assignment with his whole heart.

God doesn't speak to us in that audible voice like he did centuries ago or send his son Jesus in the flesh to deliver his message, but he instead speaks to our hearts and lets us know that he is still with us. He speaks to us through songs, through prayer, through his spirit, he speaks to us by other's ministering to us, and through his Son Jesus Christ. So, if something is tugging at you and it feels appropriate to do it, do it. Then you're hearing Christ speak to your heart. He's sending you on a mission that you can't refuse because it was written in your destiny from the moment you were born. So, if God is on your side, who can be against you?

KEY ENCOUNTER: INSPIRATIONAL IV

NOAH WARNING, "IT'S GONNA RAIN"

I'm sure that everyone is familiar the story of Noah and the flood. Are you? This dynamic biblical story tells of a man by the name of Noah. Noah was just an ordinary man walking the earth, very much like we are today. Noah was first mentioned in the bible when his father Lamech predicted the upcoming destruction of the earth and Noah's role in restoring mankind.

This was to come to past, because the people were living in destruction and the Lord had gotten tired of all the wickedness and violence that was happening, so he decided to destroy them. Noah was chosen to fulfill an assignment that had been given to him by God. He was going to be on a Mission that he really did not grasp completely, but because of who

Noah was, he just trusted the Lord and obeyed his command.........

("The Story of Noah's Ark from the Bible's Book of Genesis")

And Methuselah lived a hundred eighty and seven years, And begat Lamech. And Methuselah lived after he begat Lamech seven hundred eighty and two years and begat sons and daughters: And all the days of Methuselah were nine hundred sixty and nine years: and he died. And Lamech lived an hundred eighty and two years, and begat a son: And he called his name Noah, saying, this same shall comfort us concerning our work and toil of our hands, because of the ground which the Lord hath cursed. (Genesis 5: 25-29 KJV)

According to these scriptures, Methuselah was Noah's grandfather and Lamech the son of Methuselah was Noah's father.

The Generation of Noah and the Flood

"'These are the generations of Noah: Noah
was a just man and perfect in his generations,
and Noah walked with God. And Noah begat
three sons, Shem, Ham, and Japheth".
- Genesis 6:9-10 (KJV)

During Noah's time on earth, the earth was wicked, and God was not pleased with the way that people were living. It was filled with hatred and violence and turmoil, so God said unto Noah, that the end of all flesh is come before me, and he was going to destroy the people with the earth. God instructed Noah to build an arc of gopher wood; make rooms in it and pitch it within and without. (Meaning make it waterproof/use a waterproof material).

God was preparing for a great day by telling Noah to get this ark ready because he knew that he was going to destroy the earth and he wanted Noah and his family to be ready. God told Noah to build the ark with specific measurements so that everything could fit in it, such as he had certain dimensions for the height and width of the ark. He told Noah to place a window in the ark in a cubit above the ark, the door shall be placed in the side, with lower, second, and third stories in it.

And when the Ark is finished God told Noah that he was going to bring a great flood to destroy all flesh and everything that is in the earth shall die. He told Noah that he would establish a covenant and he will come into the ark, and his wife, his sons, and their wives. And of every living thing of all flesh, He should bring two of every sort into the ark, male and female. He told Noah to bring fowls after their kind, cattle of their kind, and every creeping thing of the earth after his kind. God told Noah to gather food for him and his family. And Noah did just as the Lord had commanded him to do.

.... Afterwards God caused a great flood to come, destroying everything and everyone except, the Ark that Noah built, what was inside the ark and his family. Noah took on a great commission when God sent him on a mission to build the Ark and save what he had commanded. I am reminded of this story, when I think about how God has chosen me, to write about his goodness and his mercy.

Whenever the Lord assigns you something to do whether great or small, you are to do it without doubt.

God does not assign us a task and leave us alone to figure it out. Through all my trials and my tribulations of uncertainty, I knew that the "Lord" was standing right beside me and that he was going to help see me through whatever endeavor I was faced with.

I have been hesitant about this assignment because I knew that it would be tedious and time consuming, but God spoke to my heart, and said you have a mission to complete, because I need you to tell somebody about your mission, so that you may be able to help someone else. God wants us to recognize him and know that he is the God, and he is God alone.

THERE'S A STORM COMING

Here's a song I wrote while I pondered and pondered what God intended Noah to say to his people. He asked Noah to warn the people that a storm was coming and that they should prepare for it since a massive flood was on the way.

This is pretty similar to how we are already conducting our lives. People are proclaiming their own gods and doing pretty much anything they want.

There's a storm coming!

There's a storm coming, Noah warned the people,
He said get ready for the day is gonna come.
When God gets ready, he gonna show up,
You've been warned, you've been warned.
God gonna pay us according to our works,
he's gonna pay us according to our works.
You better get your house in order, cause
the king of Glory, is coming soon.

Chorus: Oh, oh, yes, he is
Noah warned the people, that the storm is raging,
way out on the open sea,
He said my Lord and my savior, he's coming soon,
get your house in order, yeaaaa
he's coming soon.

Chorus: Oh, oh yes, he is
I don't know how or when,
but my Jesus is coming,
like a roaring wind, and when he comes,
He's going to pay us according to our work.

Chorus: Oh, yes, he is.

If you're on the house top you
might as well stay there,
No need to come down cause
you're not going to drown,
God promised at the day of judgement
This earth will be consumed by fire.
You better be ready
You better be ready,

So, get your house in order,
Cause like a chariot of fire,
God is coming soon.
Oh, yes, he is.

Song written by Essie M. Moore

Bible Passage

"I returned, and saw under the sun, that the race is not to the swift, nor the battle to the strong, neither yet bread to the wise, nor yet riches to men of understanding, nor yet favor to men of skill; but time and chance happened to them all". -Ecclesiastes 9:11 (KJV)

My Thoughts

This means you might not be the best in achieving the task assigned, or the one that has the most strength, or even the most knowledgeable person in the room, but God doesn't care about that, you don't have to be dressed fabulous for him, he can still use you and accomplish whatever he has assigned you to do, if you desire it from your heart. When you learn to depend on Jesus, that is when, you will learn that his grace is sufficient to see you through".

References

Publishers, Good Counsel. n.d. *The Holy Bible.* Chicago Illinois: Good Counsel Publishers, Special Edition, 1960,1963,1965, by J, G. Ferguson Publishing Company.

Moore, Essie. "There's a Storm Coming", 2021.

About the Author

Author, College Professor, Beauty Consultant, Licensed Cosmetology Instructor, and Devoted Church Worker. The Texas Cosmetology Commission's board of licensing acknowledged her as a Master in her area. She enjoys assisting others and considers it a God-given talent. She works tirelessly at it, offering free services and guidance to anyone who needs it.

Her education includes an Associates of Applied Science degree in Cosmetology, a bachelor's degree in arts and sciences, a master's degree in Education, and a doctorate in her field. She was also listed in WHO'S WHO Among Teachers and has worked at her church as a Youth and Choir Director. She identifies as a Baptist.

Her twenty years as a professional cosmetologist and dedicated church official, together with her leadership and teaching skills, have qualified her to deliver you this great information. She has had the opportunity to help people of all ages, young and old, achieve their goals by working in various positions.

Thank you for reading, and I hope you found this book, inspiring, motivating, and has been helpful as to what "God" wants you to do. Continue to be brave, strong, and courageous in your faith, and in God's Word.

God Bless,
Dr. Essie M. Moore

Printed in the United States
by Baker & Taylor Publisher Services